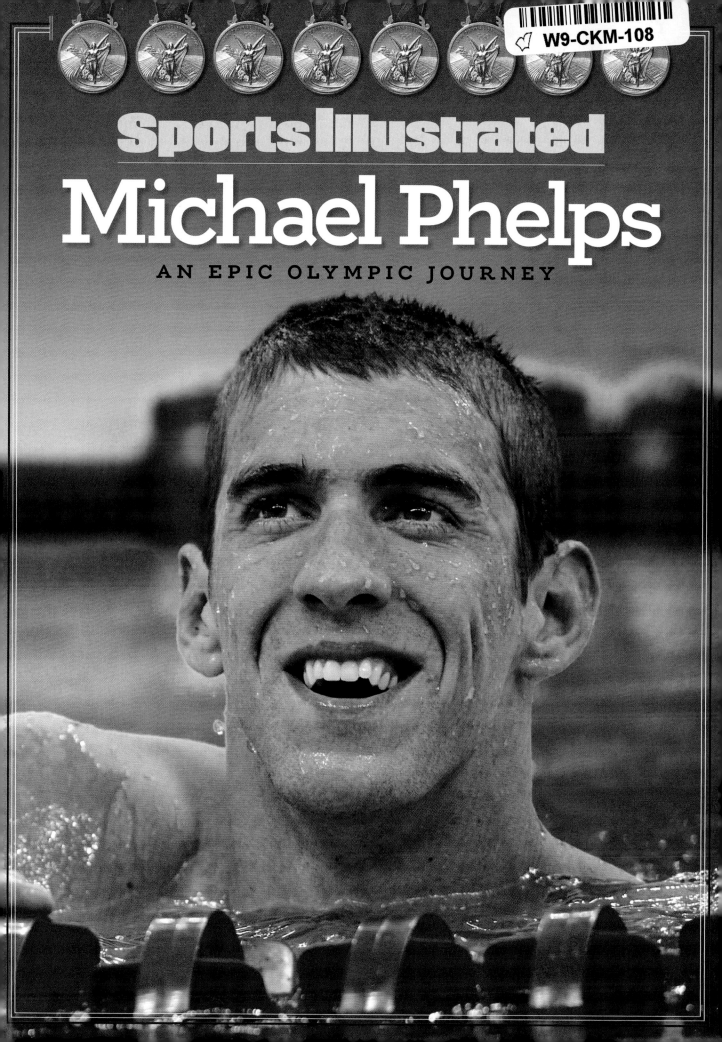

Sports Illustrated

Michael Phelps

AN EPIC OLYMPIC JOURNEY

The 400-Meter Individual Medley

©2008 Visa. All Rights Reserved.

VISA | ⬤⬤⬤⬤⬤

WORLDWIDE SPONSOR FOR OVER 20 YEARS

The 4x100-Meter Freestyle Relay

USA
JONES

USA

VISA ⬭⬭⬭⬭⬭

MICHAEL
PHE

Sports Illustrated

LPS

AN EPIC OLYMPIC JOURNEY

To contact Sports Illustrated Books, write to Sports Illustrated Books, Attention: Book Editors, PO Box 11016, Des Moines, IA 50336-1016. To order hardcover Collector's Edition books, call 1-800-327-6388 (Monday–Friday, 7:00 a.m.–8:00 p.m. or Saturday, 7:00 a.m.–6:00 p.m. Central Time). To order posters of Sports Illustrated's Aug. 25 cover of Michael Phelps (page 9) go to fineartlimited.com or call 1-800-544-5239.

The 200-Meter Freestyle

VISA | ⭕⭕⭕

WORLDWIDE SPONSOR FOR OVER 20 YEARS

Sports Illustrated C O N T E N T S

Michael Phelps ‖ AN EPIC OLYMPIC JOURNEY

Cover and Contents photographs by Heinz Kluetmeier | *Cover medal insets by* Simon Bruty

Star Turn

To help him maximize his performance, Michael Phelps has a set of eyes in the sky. His guy, USA Swimming's performance science and technology director Jonty Skinner, dissects every turn, like this one after the third length of the 400 IM. Analysis? Perfect. Phelps took gold.

Photograph by **Simon Bruty**

A Belly Full

With a nod to a popular $2 poster that featured Mark Spitz with all seven of his 1972 Olympic gold medals, SI made a cover shot of Phelps in all of his Olympic glory (page 91). These medals are inlaid with jade, and this model, of course, sports one more piece of hardware than the original.

Photograph by **Simon Bruty**

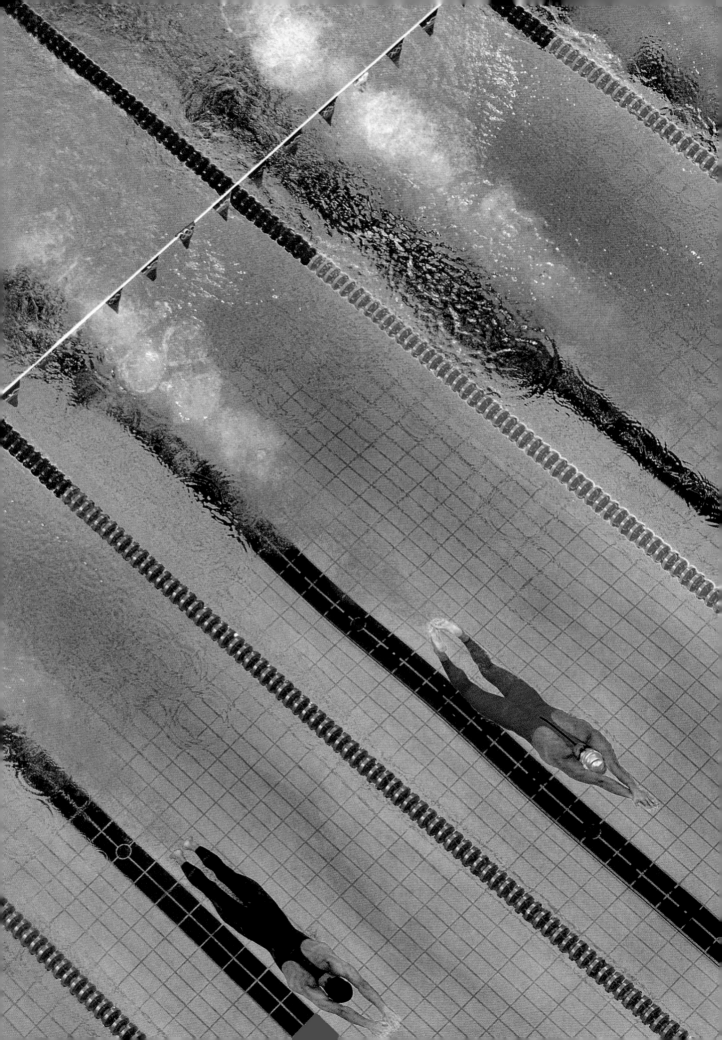

And He's Off....

From the start of his first final of the Olympics, the 400 IM, Phelps (center) took the lead and outraced Hungary's Laszlo Cseh (second from top), who is both a rival and an admirer. "It's not a shame to be beaten by a better one," said Cseh, who took silver behind Phelps here and in two later races.

Photograph by **Simon Bruty**

THE

RISE

FROM BALTIMORE TO ATHENS

Born to Swim

THE MAKING OF MICHAEL PHELPS

Inspired by a close bond with his family and his visionary coach, the once-in-a-generation phenom made his way to the 2004 Athens Olympics as a talent who left even his rivals in awe

by TIM LAYDEN

Photograph by Donald Miralle/Getty Images

I**N THE** second week of June 2004 a high school swimming pool in suburban Colorado Springs has been transformed into a soundstage as Michael Phelps films a commercial for AT&T Wireless during a break from 17 days of intense altitude swimming at the U.S. Olympic Training Center. One day training and the next day on television. Such is life on the cusp of Olympic history. In gathering darkness the 18-year-old orders a double cheeseburger from a catering truck outside the pool and then punches up an NBA playoff score on his BlackBerry. "Pistons by one, second quarter, yeah!" he says. His tousled brown hair bounces as he walks, and his baggy shorts hang below his knees.

The BlackBerry, a new acquisition, is one of the gadgets that drive him almost as much as swimming fast. "I just got an iPod," he says enthusiastically. "I put 850 songs on it, and it's *sooo* much better than carrying around a bunch of CDs." Asked whether his songs were downloaded legally or illegally, Phelps says, "I'll keep eating now," and stuffs half a burger into his mouth.

He likes to call himself a normal teenager. And he is—except for the millions of dollars in endorsement contracts, the shiny Cadillac Escalade, the starring role in NBC Olympic ads and the once-in-a-generation athletic talent. If all goes perfectly for Phelps in Athens, he will win eight gold medals, breaking swimmer Mark Spitz's Olympic record of seven. If Phelps has an off meet, he is still almost certain to take home more medals than any of the Games' 10,000 other competitors.

The sport has rarely seen an athlete so gifted. Phelps, who is 6' 4" with a pterodactyl's wingspan of 76½ inches, is blessed with almost unprecedented versatility—he is exceptional at butterfly, backstroke, freestyle and individual medley, composed of those three strokes plus the breaststroke—and has an instinctive grasp of the medium in which he competes. "He just *feels* the water," says training partner and former Auburn All-America Kevin Clements. "He knows exactly where to put his hand so that it doesn't make any bubbles. Every stroke is perfect."

Even fellow world-record holders marvel at him. Says Olympic favorite Aaron Peirsol, the only person ever to have swum the 200-meter backstroke faster than Phelps, "He has a gift, man. A physical and mental gift. To be able to do all those different strokes, obviously his brain functions differently from most people's."

The Games will not decide whether Phelps is wealthy or poor. His sponsor deals guarantee him an annual income comfortably into seven figures through 2009. (Speedo first signed him in '01, when he was 16; he became the company's youngest-ever male endorser.) The Olympics will decide, however, whether Phelps becomes more than just an outstanding swimmer with a sharp

EMERGING STAR
At the 2000 spring nationals the 14-year-old Phelps broke the two-minute barrier in the 200 fly, prompting Bowman to predict he'd make Sydney.

agent. They will test whether he can transcend his sport and become one of the Olympics' alltime greats.

They will also measure his ability to take the biggest athletic spectacle on earth and carry it on his broad shoulders. The drug scandal that has engulfed track and field has thrust swimming to the forefront of the Games. "The BALCO case has been awful for track, because companies won't touch that sport right now," says Evan Morgenstein, agent for more than two dozen world-class swimmers, "but it's been a windfall for swimming."

NBC began promoting Phelps months ago, putting his dripping face on the screen during the Kentucky Derby and golf's U.S. Open. "Let's face it," says Spitz, no stranger to the vagaries of Olympic fame. "Michael is NBC's meal ticket."

Phelps first opened eyes by making the 2000 Olympic team just 10 weeks after his 15th birthday and by breaking the 200-meter butterfly record seven months later to become the youngest male world-record holder in history. He soon became the first swimmer to win U.S. titles in backstroke, butterfly, freestyle and both IMs. But what lifted him into truly rarefied air was his performance at the '03 world championships in Barcelona, where he set five world records and won six medals, four of them gold.

That tour de force not only earned Phelps the Sullivan Award as the nation's best amateur athlete in '03 but also raised the possibility of his challenging Spitz's Olympic record—a topic that has shadowed Phelps for the past year. "His name comes up in every interview, guaranteed," Phelps says of Spitz, whom he had never met until last month's U.S. trials. "That's O.K. He was the man, the icon."

The parallels between the two swimmers are limited. In 1972 Spitz was a former college superstar (at Indiana) who had already won two gold medals in Olympic competition and had a reputation for cockiness. Phelps is just a year out of Towson (Md.) High (he has deferred his college plans) and finished fifth in the 200 butterfly in Sydney. While he does not lack for confidence or style, he tempers his public image with a big kid's mellow cool.

WONDER YEARS
Getting his feet wet at the North Baltimore Aquatic Club at age eight helped Phelps hone the skills needed to qualify for Sydney as a 15-year-old (right) at the '00 Olympic trials.

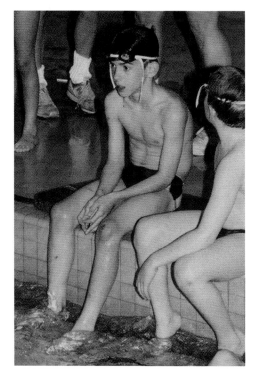

Moreover, Phelps's Olympic swimming schedule is more varied, and arguably more difficult, than Spitz's was in '72. "Mark swam the freestyle and butterfly, which are the two most technically similar strokes, and he swam 100 and 200 meters, which are virtually the same event," says 1976 Olympic champion John Naber. "Also, the U.S. relays were almost guaranteed to win three gold medals in those days."

Phelps will use all four strokes to cover distances from 100 to 400 meters, and two of the three relay teams on which he's expected to compete won't even be clear favorites. He'll swim 17 races (Spitz swam 13) in eight days and enter five individual events (Spitz swam four). On Aug. 19 Phelps will have to swim the 100-meter butterfly semifinals just 21 minutes after he finishes the 200 IM final. And whereas Spitz entered the Munich Games as the world-record holder in all of his events, Phelps holds world marks in three of his (the 200 and 400 IMs and the 200 butterfly) and is ranked No. 2 in the world in the others (100 fly and 200 freestyle). "It's going to be a tough Olympics program for Michael," says Ian Thorpe, Australia's swimming superstar, who'll face Phelps in multiple races.

Spitz knows that better than anyone. "I think Michael is capable of winning seven, just like I was capable of winning seven," he says. "But a lot of things had to happen just right for me. And the U.S. relays were unquestionably stronger in 1972, relative to the competition. I hope he does it. It would be great for the sport and great for Michael. And it's already been great press for me that he's trying."

Phelps has never publicly professed his desire to win seven gold medals. In a carefully planned posture, he will admit only to chasing one. "To stand up on that podium and hear the national anthem would be awesome," he says. "Swimming has changed a lot since Spitz's day. People specialize more. So for me it's win one gold medal, and after that, whatever happens, happens."

Calculated or not, that attitude befits Phelps, who is trying to not get swept up in the trappings of fame and fortune. He has been surrounded by the same core of close friends since he was in fourth grade, guys like Matt Townsend (a student at Salisbury State) and Ayo Osho (Maryland). Like Phelps, they love the Ravens and hate the Yankees.

"We play Texas hold 'em but not for money," Townsend says. "We play Xbox and PS2. Sometimes we just hang out and watch movies. He's a great friend. There's no way anyone would know that he's somebody famous, with all these world records." Pause. "Of course I stayed over at his house the other night, and by the time I got out of bed, he was already coming back from his [7 a.m.] workout."

FOG DANCES across the surface of the pool, 20 minutes past sunset in mid-June. Trees sway in the cool wind. A long day of age-group racing is nearly finished at the Meadowbrook Swim Club in North Baltimore when Phelps climbs atop a starting block to swim the anchor leg of the men's open 400-meter freestyle relay, the final event. Dozens of children and parents crowd the side of the pool to watch the would-be Olympic hero in his final tune-up before the U.S. trials.

He has been coming to this pool since age five. It was here that he scampered about, begging snacks from swim moms while his two older sisters trained and raced. It was here that he blossomed into a prodigy at 10, crushing older swimmers yet enduring their taunts about his outsized ears, which he tucked beneath baseball caps—one Michigan (a school he grew up wanting to attend), one Orioles. It was here that Phelps watched his sister Whitney, five years older than he, rise to the favorite's role at age 15 for the 1996 Olympic trials, only to miss the team, a disappointment that he says left the family devastated. And it was here that his new coach, Bob Bowman, met with divorced parents Fred and Debbie Phelps in the fall of '97 and told them that their 12-year-old son could someday swim in the Olympics.

The family's devotion to the sport had started before Michael was born. Debbie Phelps was the stay-at-home mom of two small girls in Maryland's rural Harford County, on the Pennsylvania border. Fred, her high school sweetheart and a onetime defensive back at Fairmont State College in West Virginia, was a Maryland state policeman and often worked swing shifts. On the recommendation of her pediatrician, Debbie started the girls, seven-year-old Hilary and

A MOTHER'S LOVE
The connection between Debbie and Michael (left, at the National Aquarium in Baltimore in '04) was strengthened after his parents' 1995 divorce.

five-year-old Whitney, swimming, and they took to it like mermaids. Born just as the girls began to race, Michael spent countless hours riding in the back of the family car to training sessions and races. He started swimming when he was seven but resisted getting his face wet, so he stuck to backstroke.

Whitney was the swimmer with early promise. She swam on a world-championship team at 14 and was ranked No. 1 in the U.S. in the 200 butterfly entering the 1996 Olympic trials. However, she had been fighting soreness in her back for months before the event. "I was telling people, 'No, it doesn't hurt,' but I was walking around like an 80-year-old woman," she says. "But get out of the pool? Never. You don't want to be a wimp." She finished sixth at the trials.

Michael remembers the heartbreak of his sister's crushing disappointment. Debbie can't discuss it without crying. Hilary says, "Nobody talks about '96. It's the elephant in the room for our family."

It was the type of experience that could have soured the family on supporting another child in the sport. But it did not. Later that year Bowman was hired as coach of the North Baltimore Aquatic Club. He inherited Michael, a short, skinny kid with uncanny presence in the water. Within a year Bowman suggested to Debbie and Fred that their son might someday make the Olympics and therefore should consider dumping baseball and lacrosse. Michael resisted. "You're ruining my life!" he told Bowman one afternoon during eighth grade, when the coach suggested adding morning workouts. "I'm spending 90 percent of my time at the pool."

Bowman backed off and implemented the double sessions a year later, when Phelps was more mature, and the work paid off. In a preliminary swim at the spring national championships outside Seattle in March 2000, Phelps lowered his 200 butterfly personal best by an astonishing five seconds, to 1:59 flat. The time instantly made him one of the fastest swimmers in the world, at age 14. "It was the most boring environment you could imagine," says Bowman. "There were maybe two people in the stands. There was no cheering. Then Michael swims 1:59. I remember walking to my car after that swim, stopping and saying out loud, 'He's going to make the Olympic team.' That day changed everything."

Phelps went to the 2000 Olympic trials as a dark horse in the 200 fly, and he didn't go alone. Whitney had continued to swim in pain, just well enough to earn a scholarship to UNLV, and had qualified in the same stroke and distance. "Good enough to qualify, not good enough to make it anymore," she says of her decision to pull out of the race because of a bulging disk in her neck. But when Michael stunned the swimming world by making the team with a second-place finish, she greeted him on the pool deck with a lingering hug. "Huge," says Michael of the embrace. "So huge."

"I just went with my feelings that day," says Whitney. "It was an amazing thing for a male swimmer that age to make the Olympic team. And he's my little brother; he means the world to me."

High above the water, Debbie wept. She and Michael have always been close, but their bond had gotten stronger after Debbie and Fred's 1995 divorce. "She has always been there for me," says Michael. "She's done everything. We're best friends." On Mother's Day morning Michael instructed Debbie to watch a TV interview in which he emotionally described her place in his life and ended by saying, "Thanks, Mom." When he returned to Maryland from Colorado in mid-June, he delivered Slurpees to the office where she works as a school administrator.

Fred Phelps, who retired in February 2004 after 28 years, says, "Michael and I were close when he was little. We went to games together, we hit baseballs, did all the things that fathers and sons do. When Debbie and I divorced, there were some tough years. I know what it's like; my dad died when I was eight." Father and son trade regular e-mails, but Michael says, "Right now is when I don't need anything new in my life."

ON A COLD, gray morning in December 2003, Phelps arrived at the Meadowbrook pool to find that Bowman had assigned him a crushing set of 50 100-meter, kick-only sprints. Phelps climbed into the pool and began moving slowly. Bowman shouted at him, "You might as well not even bother!" Phelps, holding a kickboard, shouted back at Bowman, and before long Phelps was in his Escalade, headed back home. "I don't even remember whether I quit or got kicked out," says Phelps.

SWIM TEAM
Bowman put Phelps through 12-mile-a-day workouts for almost three years before Athens, polishing his prodigy into a nearly perfect sleek swimming machine.

It was a rare hiccup in a four-year plan that relied heavily on Phelps's uncommon drive and maturity. Athletically, Phelps is a freak, with what 1984 gold medalist Rowdy Gaines calls "the perfect body for swimming: long arms, big hands and feet, short legs yet long torso."

On top of that, Phelps finds motivation at every turn. Since the 2003 worlds he has kept on his bedroom wall a photograph of U.S. rival Ian Crocker, who beat him in the 100 fly final and took away his world record. When Thorpe's coach suggested last winter that Phelps was incapable of matching Spitz's seven golds, Phelps says, "It fired me up." Phelps is also fueled by slights from the past. Nearly two years ago a young man approached him at a meet and congratulated him on his accomplishments, adding, "Do you remember me? I used to swim against you?" In fact, he was one of the 13-year-olds who used to make fun of Phelps's big ears and skinny body.

"Sorry," Phelps said, "I don't remember you." Later he told Hilary, "Of course I remember him. But the way he treated me, there's no way I was going to give him the satisfaction."

Phelps and Bowman have an almost symbiotic relationship. For nearly three years following Sydney, Bowman put Phelps through long-distance training, sometimes more than 12 miles a day. This year the load has lessened slightly, with greater emphasis on quality and stroke adjustment. The results have been promising. During a mid-June training session in Colorado Springs, Phelps swam five 200-meter frees with minimal rest, the last in a searing 1:51.9, nearly three seconds faster than usual for a similar workout, despite the thin air. At the trials—a meet for which he didn't fully rest or taper—he set one world record and won four of the six events in which he qualified. "You have to be prepared to break the world record every time you swim against him," says Australia's Justin Norris, who expects to face Phelps in both IMs and the 200 butterfly in Athens.

"Everything I've done for two years has pointed toward this summer," says Phelps as he stands by the side of the pool in Baltimore, bathed in twilight. In May the pool was drained for a black-tie dinner at which Phelps was the guest of honor. Now he wears a gray hoodie over sopping hair, a weary teenager with big dreams. Athens beckons, and with it a place in Olympic history, with one gold medal or many more. □

SIMON BRUTY (RIGHT); DOUG PENSINGER/GETTY IMAGES

2001 *World Championships*

MAKING RIPPLES

The Olympics caught a brief peek of Phelps at the 2000 Games in Sydney, but it wasn't until the '01 worlds that the modest 16-year-old caused the swimming community to stand up and take notice

by BRIAN CAZENEUVE

Photograph by Mark Baker/Reuters

AT THE world swimming championships in Fukuoka, Japan, on July 27, 2001, Michael Phelps sat in the pressroom of the Marine Messe arena and eyed a newsletter headline that read WORLD RECORDS FOR TEENAGE SENSATIONS IAN THORPE AND MICHAEL PHELPS. Sure, Phelps, 16, had just swum 1:54.58 to shatter the world mark in the 200-meter butterfly for the second time in four months, but to share top billing with a legend, albeit a contemporary one, was to be in uncharted waters. "Awesome," Phelps crowed. "He's, like, all-world."

And all-worldly. Thorpe, 18, shed his teenage awkwardness long ago. He hired an agent at 14, became a Qantas spokesman at 15, met the Australian prime minister at 16, won five Olympic medals in Sydney at 17 and recently started a foundation to aid disadvantaged children. Thorpe comports himself with a confidence and sophistication beyond that of most adults, and he can swim a little too. In Fukuoka he set personal bests in each of the seven events he entered, won six gold medals—the most ever at a world championships—and broke world records in four events (the 200-meter freestyle, 400 free, 800 free and 4 × 200 free relay). In the 4 × 100 free relay Thorpe, swimming the anchor leg for Australia, overcame a deficit of nearly a body length in the last 30 meters to edge Anthony Ervin of the U.S.

Since the Olympics, Thorpe has attended parties for Giorgio Armani and Jennifer Lopez, met Queen Elizabeth, visited the Royal Palace in Monte Carlo and accepted an invitation to see Chelsea Clinton, who had told him in Sydney, "If you're ever in Washington. . . ."

There were no snazzy invites for Phelps after he set his first world record in the 200 fly, 1:54.92, at the U.S. nationals in Austin in March. He returned home to Baltimore and wanted to celebrate with his sister Hilary at a local Cheesecake Factory. Told there was a two-hour wait, they moved on, unwilling to try to play the celebrity card. "I couldn't have," says Phelps, a junior at Towson (Md.) High. "Outside my school, people don't know who I am. It doesn't compare, me and Thorpe."

It does in some ways. With his race in Austin, the swimmer who has been called the U.S. answer to Thorpe supplanted Thorpe as the youngest male swimmer ever to set a world record. Both teens have mothers who are schoolteachers and older sisters who made their national swim teams. Both wear their success modestly.

There the parallels end. Thorpe has made millions from swimming, through contracts with Adidas, Coke and Omega, and has had his nickname, Thorpedo, trademarked. Phelps is still an amateur (though that may change soon). At 15 Thorpe won his first car; at 16 Phelps is waiting to get his learner's permit. Thorpe fancies films; Phelps prefers PlayStation.

A post-teen rivalry is conceivable, because Phelps swims the 400-meter individual medley and Thorpe may one day add that to his repertoire. "The advice I would give Michael is not to limit your expectations by your age," says Thorpe. "It's a great time learning the person you'll become, so enjoy it." □

ALL-WORLDLY
In '01 Phelps got a first-hand look at Thorpe (above), the presumed greatest swimmer ever. Since then Phelps has changed a few minds.

DONALD MIRALLE/GETTY IMAGES

Ascendant in Athens

ADMIRERS IN HIS WAKE

Michael Phelps's gold rush at the 2004 Games hit a couple of bronze bumps, but he won races and friends, proving himself the world's most versatile swimmer—and an all-around good guy

by KELLI ANDERSON

Photograph by Simon Bruty

COULD THIS have been the defining Olympic moment for Michael Phelps? After seven days and 17 races Phelps had won five gold and two bronze medals in the Athens pool. One more of any color would make him the first person to win eight medals in a single, nonboycotted Games. So where was the celebrated 19-year-old from Baltimore when his eighth and final event was about to begin on the evening of Aug. 21? He was in the stands in team-issued street clothes, waving an American flag and finally enjoying a day off from swimming. Because he had swum the preliminary round in the medley relay, Phelps would be awarded whatever medal the U.S. won, so his historic moment was in the hands of four other guys, and he was going to lead the cheers.

The night before, in what U.S. men's coach Eddie Reese would call "a hell of a gesture," Phelps had given up his spot in that final, one he had openly coveted and had earned by winning the 100 butterfly. He offered the spot to Ian Crocker, the man who had cost him a shot at tying Mark Spitz's single-Games record of seven gold medals by swimming a disastrously slow opening leg in the 4 × 100 freestyle relay earlier in the week. "Ian's one of the greatest relay swimmers in history," said Phelps. "I was willing to give him another chance."

The other three swimmers on the medley relay final had not enjoyed a seamless Olympics either. Brendan Hansen, the world-record holder in both breaststroke races, had failed to beat his rival, Kosuke Kitajima of Japan, in either event. Backstroker Aaron Peirsol had publicly accused Kitajima of using an illegal dolphin kick in the 100 breast, and four days later, in what some suspected was payback, Peirsol was disqualified after winning the 200 backstroke by over two seconds when a judge deemed one of his turns illegal. The DQ was quickly overturned, but relay anchor Jason Lezak's shocking result would not vanish so easily. Like Crocker, Lezak had failed to make the 100 freestyle semifinals, leaving the U.S. without a representative in a nonboycotted 100 free final for the first time in history.

If Crocker initially found Phelps's gesture "a gift too large to accept," he had reconsidered by the time he shot off the blocks on the third leg of the relay. Capitalizing on a cushion built first by Peirsol, who broke the 100-backstroke world record he had long pursued, and then Hansen, who swam the second-fastest breaststroke split in history, Crocker churned through the water in 50.28, the second-fastest fly split ever. After Lezak touched in a world-record time of 3:30.68, Crocker collected his only gold medal of the meet and then found Phelps for a brief embrace. "He said, 'Congratulations,' and I said, 'Thank you,'" said the laconic Crocker. "He gave me a great opportunity."

For the U.S. team it was a happy conclusion to what had been a week of ups and downs. The only constant was Phelps, who turned in one personal-best

PERFECT DAY
The Athens Games got off to a fast start for Phelps (fifth from left), who won gold and set a world record in the first event, the 400 IM.

THORPEDOED

Phelps's chances for eight golds were all washed up after the U.S. team lost the 4×100 relay and he finished third behind Thorpe (yellow cap) and Pieter van den Hoogenband of the Netherlands in the 200-meter freestyle.

performance after another, sometimes with just a few deep breaths and his customary postrace Carnation Instant Breakfast to sustain him between races. His wins in the 400 and 200 individual medleys and the 100 and 200 butterflies tied Spitz's record of four individual gold medals by a swimmer in one Olympics. But Phelps's most riveting race was the 4 × 200 freestyle relay. After creating a body-length lead over defending Olympic champion Australia on the first leg, Phelps stood behind the blocks transfixed as one teammate after another held off a charge from the Aussies. When Klete Keller of the U.S. out-touched 200-free world-record holder Ian Thorpe, Phelps went uncharacteristically bonkers, raising his arms high and adding his triumphant yell to the din around him. "That was the most exciting race I have ever been a part of," he said later. "I don't think I have ever celebrated like that in my life."

ONE FOR THE TEAM
After earning seven trips to the podium, Phelps (above) took to the stands as spectator, giving teammate Crocker a chance at redemption, which he turned into gold.

The women's 4 × 200 free relay provided another high for the U.S. With Natalie Coughlin leading off with a leg that would have won the 200 free, an event she didn't enter in Athens, the U.S. smashed the oldest Olympic swimming record on the books, set in '87 by East German swimmers who were part of a sports program that former GDR officials have admitted was fueled by performance enhancing drugs.

As the winner of eight medals Phelps now belongs to a special class, the only other member of which is Aleksandr Dityatin, a Soviet gymnast who won three golds, four silvers and a bronze at the boycotted 1980 Olympics. "There's nobody in the last 20 years, in any sport, who can say they did what Michael did this week," says Reese. "He was born to swim, and he has great talent, great versatility and great resiliency. And he does the hardest workouts in the world. You don't beat that combination until he retires."

Don't expect that to happen soon. When his sixth gold medal finally reaches him via mail, several weeks hence, Phelps will certainly be in the pool, already thinking about making another run at Spitz's record seven golds in Beijing. □

The College Days

DEEP BLUE

Aside from being a six-time gold medalist and the world's best swimmer, Michael Phelps was just like any other freshman at the University of Michigan in 2005

by BRIAN CAZENEUVE

Photograph by Heinz Kluetmeier

O N HIS first visit to Zingerman's, the downtown Ann Arbor hot spot that eventually lures nearly every Michigan undergrad to sample one of its famously overstuffed sandwiches, Michael Phelps is eyeing the 50-plus choices on an overhead menu when a female employee's hand taps his shoulder. "Excuse me, but I just have to ask: Michael Phelps, right?"

"Yup, right," he answers pleasantly.

"There's a girl who usually works in here. She'd go crazy if you could sign something for her. Could you?"

"Sure, no problem."

Moments later, as Phelps sits at a back table waiting for a waitress to bring over his ambitious selection (Tarb's Tenacious Tenure), a man at the adjacent table turns to tap Phelps's shoulder. "Sorry to bother you," he says, "but are you Michael Phelps?" The 19-year-old Olympic medalist nods. "My son is a swimmer," the man continues. "He has a big meet coming up this weekend, and if you wished him luck, he would just, just . . . um, here's a napkin you can sign."

"Sure, no problem."

At that Phelps's challenge finally arrives in front of him, a heaping pile of turkey and Muenster popping out from underneath thick grilled farm bread. "You're kidding," Phelps says in astonishment. He studies the colossus as if it were a tricky science project—flipping it, rotating it, finding just the right angle—before finally attacking it. Upon taking a bite, Phelps, with dressing still dripping from his mouth, is transformed from an internationally recognized athlete to an ordinary student. "I didn't know what to expect coming here," he says of Michigan. "New place, new friends. But I really like it."

In April 2004, while prepping his protégé for the Athens Olympics, Phelps's coach, Bob Bowman, agreed to take over the men's swimming program at the U of M. Phelps followed his coach to Ann Arbor, where he is a volunteer assistant for the swim team and began taking classes in January '05. As a professional, he is not eligible to compete for the Wolverines.

Though Phelps often tucks his head under a baseball cap and dresses as informally as any other college student, it's hard for him to go to class or grab lunch without standing out. "When a teacher had us introduce ourselves on the first day of classes, I remember all the heads turning when my name was called. I just said, 'Hi, I'm Michael,' " he says. "I'm trying to play it low-pro." Phelps is majoring in sports management, a logical choice since he has talked of becoming either an agent or an event promoter when his swimming days are up. To leave time for making appearances around the country, he is taking only two classes in his first semester, both meeting on Tuesday and Thursday mornings: Historical and Sociological Bases of Human Movement and Public Interpersonal Communications.

The public-speaking course is a layup for Phelps, who has already spoken before dozens of charity groups, held more

IN HIS ELEMENT
No Photoshop here. SI dropped a desk, computer and all the rest into Michigan's Canham Natatorium to get below the surface with Phelps.

than 100 press conferences and twice appeared on *The Tonight Show.* On this day he is asked to speak briefly on a random subject—which turns out to be sleep, something with which he is very familiar.

"I, um, do sports in the mornings and afternoons," he begins, sending the class into laughter at his attempt at modesty, "so rest is very important because it allows me to recuperate and get ready for my next class or my next training session." A poised Phelps aces the drill. The other students commend him for his clarity, smile, good hand gestures and relaxed body movement. One student does cite him for using verbal fillers—one *um* and two *uh*'s—and as he leaves class, Phelps quietly chides himself. "Did I really say 'uh' twice?" he asks.

MICHIGAN MAN
As a pro Phelps couldn't compete for the Wolverines, but he went to Ann Arbor to train with Bowman (blue sweater), his longtime coach.

After lunch Phelps takes a power nap. He has quite the digs for it: a four-story town house that is within walking distance of campus. Being a homeowner has put his domestic skills to the test. Unable to wedge a box spring up the staircase, he sleeps on a thin mattress that lies directly on the cold floor. On his first day in the house he bought milk and cereal before realizing that he owned neither bowls nor spoons. "So I mixed it all up in a Gatorade bottle," he says, "and drank the cereal from the bottle." Phelps bought a dishwasher and a washing machine but soon discovered that hand soap is not a suitable substitute for detergent, especially when suds start spilling onto the floor and turn your kitchen into a bubble bath.

"At least I'm trying," he says. "I know not to mix colors in the laundry, and I've started cooking for myself, though the steak I made the other day was kind of chewy." His pantry is well stocked, much like a 7-Eleven, with chips, pretzels, Twizzlers, fruit, snacks, cookies, PowerBars and granola bars. There are TVs on three of the four floors, and he brought 150 DVDs with him from Baltimore, including his favorite, *Miracle.* He hosted his mother and sisters over Christmas, and he's held a *Madden* football tournament for friends in his living room. But the ladies are out of luck: Though he may be the biggest man on this campus of 39,000, Phelps reports that he is off the market.

After a well-publicized DUI incident in November '04, Phelps says he has no interest in typical after-hours activities. "I learned from my mistake," he says. With two-a-day practices starting at 6 a.m., Phelps hasn't had much time for the Michigan party scene. The football scene is another matter. Phelps attended his first home game on Oct. 30, against archrival Michigan State, and later traveled to Southern California to watch the Wolverines' one-point loss to Texas in the Rose Bowl. "This place is awesome on football Saturdays," he says. "The whole town shuts down for the game."

While a blizzard pelted Ann Arbor in January, Phelps swam four exhibition races during the breaks of a Michigan diving meet. With a Donald B. Canham Natatorium–record 1,400 people in the stands, Phelps broke three pool records, even though he is not in top condition. The Wolverines swimmers do not regularly seek out advice from the world's best, but Bowman sees Phelps's impact on the team. "Michael lifts the whole level of practices," Bowman says, "and he helps other swimmers get psyched up for races. He still has a ways to go before he gets back into heavy competition." For that Phelps is eyeing the world championship trials in Indianapolis in two months, just before he tackles final exams and presentations.

Until then the Olympic star can enjoy life as a typical college freshman, learning his way around sandwiches and dishwashers. As he walks out of practice, Phelps yawns, does a double take and then tries to leap over a three-foot-high snow pile in order to get to his car. He comes up short, leaving snow stuck in his moccasins and running up his legs. "I really do own socks," he says. "I'm just too lazy to put them on. Hey, I'm in college now." □

The 200-Meter Butterfly

VISA

WORLDWIDE SPONSOR FOR OVER 20 YEARS

The 4x200-Meter Freestyle Relay

WORLDWIDE SPONSOR FOR OVER 20 YEARS

BEIJ

INTO THE BLUE
For nine days in Beijing the Water Cube bubbled with intrigue as more than 10,000 spectators asked the same question: Can Michael Phelps do it?

Photograph by Greg Baker/AP

ING
THE IMPROBABLE DREAM

Eight

THE QUEST

Long before he accomplished his unprecedented feat in Beijing, Michael Phelps was preparing, both in the pool and out. Here is the story of what he did, in eight parts

by SUSAN CASEY

Photographs by Simon Bruty

I. THE SWIMMER

Belmont Plaza is an unlovely pool, a beige hulk squatting on a grimy stretch of Long Beach in Southern California. Behind it, on the Pacific horizon, container ships and oil derricks mar the sunset. Across the parking lot a diner called Chuck's displays a sign declaring itself HOME OF THE WEASEL. In the world of sports venues, this is a long way from Beijing's Water Cube, the Olympic swimming complex designed to look as though it's made of glowing bubbles. And yet on this January night, Belmont has all the glamour. In the chlorinated half-light, Michael Phelps stands behind lane 4 adjusting a pair of black goggles, and he's about to do something amazing. Again.

Phelps, 23, is the world's greatest swimmer. Describing his career requires superlatives that haven't been invented, so let's stick with numbers: When he was 15, he competed in the Sydney Games, the youngest U.S. male Olympian since 1932. He finished fifth in the 200-meter butterfly—not bad for his first international meet. The next March, still three months from his 16th birthday, he swam the event again at U.S. nationals and broke the world record, making him the youngest male swimmer ever to own one. Through the 2008 Olympic trials, 24 more world records followed, with Phelps breaking his own 200 butterfly mark five times, once lowering it by an astonishing 1.62 seconds. He won six gold medals at the Athens Games and seven at the '07 world championships in Melbourne, and now the talk is of eight golds in Beijing. (Not that anybody's counting, but eight in Beijing would be one more than Mark Spitz won in Munich in '72.)

First, though, there is the Toyota Southern California Grand Prix at Belmont Plaza.

Phelps shrugs off his black North Face puffa and removes the hip-hop mainline from his ears. This is a short-course meet, and the pool is only 25 yards long rather than the Olympic size of 50 meters. Short course is intimate and showy; long course is imposing and grand—the traditional distance of world records. As the fastest qualifier, Phelps is introduced last, and as he steps onto the block he snaps his arms across his chest three times, a prerace ritual. Even though he's sporting a new Fu Manchu mustache, the scene is very familiar.

Except for one thing: This is the finals of the 100 breaststroke.

It's Phelps's Achilles' heel, an event he never competes in. And next to him, in lane 5, is U.S. Olympian Mark Gangloff, whose best event happens to be, well, this one. Like all sports, swimming has its unwritten rules. Here's one: You can win the 100 breaststroke or the 100 freestyle (which Phelps had done earlier in the meet), but you can't win them both. In elite competition the same person has never come close to taking these two events, and for good reason. Of the four strokes—butterfly, backstroke, breaststroke and freestyle—breaststroke is the bastard child. It's lateral where the others are linear, a specialist's choreography of power legs, tricky timing and subtle hand position. Breaststrokers and sprint freestylers have about as much in common as kangaroos and leopards.

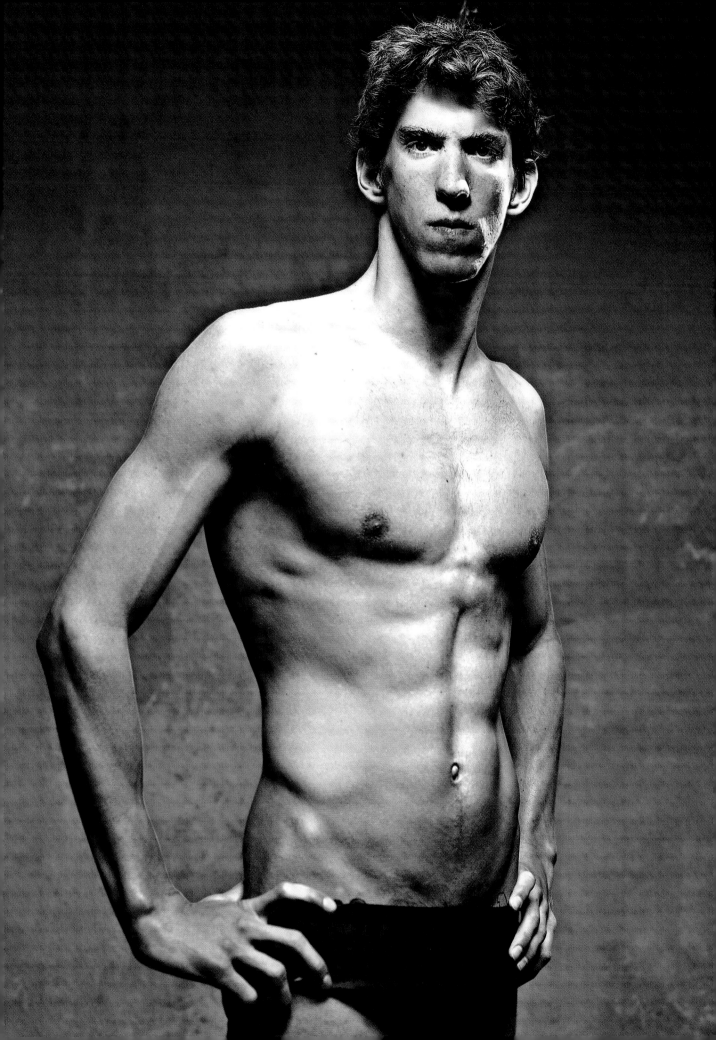

Phelps bends into his start. He's 6' 4" and has size 14 feet that are so flexible, his toes actually wrap around the edges of the block. The starter bleeps, and the field explodes; when Phelps surfaces, he's almost at the opposite wall.

His race is over in 53.41 seconds, Phelps touched out by Gangloff's 53.09. At poolside a pale-haired, midsized man wearing a navy polo shirt and wire-rimmed glasses stands with arms crossed. His face bears no emotion; he's simply watching so hard you can hear the gears whirring. This is Bob Bowman, 43, Phelps's coach. As Phelps vaults from the water and heads to the warm-down pool, Bowman's mouth curls into a Cheshire-cat smile. Yes, his athlete lost a race. But everything's relative. Tonight, by almost beating one of the world's best breaststrokers, Phelps has served notice that unlike any other swimmer in history, he no longer has a weak stroke.

"That's one of the most impressive things I've ever seen him do," Bowman says, looking at the clock.

II. THE SPORT

Picture the winter predawn, sometime in January. Somewhere in the East, like Baltimore (where Phelps began his career) or Ann Arbor, Mich. (where he trains now). It's cold, for one thing. And dark. And when the alarm clock shrieks its owner awake at 5 a.m., his bed has never felt so warm. For swimmers, nothing epitomizes their sport so much as the feeling of diving into frigid water before sunrise. The serious ones do it most mornings of their careers. Later in the day, they're back for another two or three hours. Anything else—school, what passes for a social life—is arranged around these workouts.

For nonswimmers, the idea of spending that much time going back and forth, staring at the black line on the bottom of the pool as the chlorine eats into your skin, is the definition of hellish monotony. But the swimmers aren't bored.

It's not that they're unfamiliar with the concept of repetition. Rather, it's that they can swim or kick or pull their laps; they can do it with paddles, fins, buoys, weights or surgical tubing; over any distance, on any interval and in any combination of the above. And there are four strokes to think about, each as technical as dressage—and that's before they consider starts and turns, where the closest races are decided. ("Michael basically lost the 200 free in Athens on turns," Bowman says.) The fine-tuning is endless. "Right now I'm working on fixing my head position in freestyle," Phelps says. "It's too high. Even after 11 years, I have never swum it right. I'm still working on little things that are going to make a huge difference."

III. THE COACH

Ten o'clock on a mid-April night, and Chicago's Palmer House hotel is lit up, with media members milling in the bars, Olympians giving interviews and USOC

officials checking names off lists. Beijing is less than four months away, and here is a last chance to interview the athletes whom, come August, America will suddenly want to know about. Which is to say, it's a final crack at Phelps. At a press conference earlier, one female reporter had asked him, "Can you give me two exercises people can do to get a swimmer's-type body?"

"Well . . . they could swim."

"After this I go to blackout mode," Phelps says, walking through the lobby with Bowman. "No one can get hold of me. I don't have to worry about anything, and I have no commitments—that's my favorite part. I just attend to what's coming up."

Before the bliss of Olympic immersion, however, Phelps is headed to Colorado Springs for one last brutality: a training camp at 6,000-foot altitude with several Bowman swimmers. "Seventy practices in 24 days," Phelps says. "By the end, we're at each other's throats. You learn to steer clear of people, there's so much emotion going on."

With that scenario in mind, it seems fitting that Bowman, conductor of this orchestra of pain, minored in music composition and majored in developmental psychology at Florida State. "Michael hates my sets," he acknowledges. Why? "They're hard. And the ones I like the most are the most painful." Phelps agrees: "My teammate Erik [Vendt] and I look at each other and go, God, not this one. You've got to be kidding me! *What's he trying to do to us?*"

If you went into a lab and mixed up the ingredients for the ideal coach, you'd invent someone like Bow-man. A talented swimmer in college, he quit because he was driving himself nuts with his own incessant performance critiques. "I was coaching myself all the time," he recalls. *"Well, I should've done this,* and *I could've done this better. . . ."* At the same time, he loved everything about the sport. Moving to the deck was a logical segue; Bowman inhaled what technical material he could get his hands on—not much in 1986—and then looked around for more. His eye landed on Paul Bergen, the coach who'd developed Tracy Caulkins, still considered by many the best all-around women's swimmer in U.S. history.

"I thought, This is a guy who knows what he's doing," Bowman recalls. "I wanted to work with him, but after the 1988 Olympics he quit coaching to train racehorses." What to do? Well, if you're Bowman, you travel to Napa Valley, buy a pair of knee-high boots and head for the stables.

"I'd clean the stalls and ask him about swimming," Bowman says, noting that along the way he also got hooked on horses. He currently owns and trains nine thoroughbreds. "The horses have taught me to be a better observer," he says, "because they can't tell you what they're feeling."

Phelps, however, can. As they wait to be seated in the hotel restaurant, Phelps is asked what it's like to swim 5,000 meters (more than three miles) for time, one of Bowman's semiregular requests. His face turns stony.

"I do *not* do that anymore. I can't. . . . I'm not. Those days are bye-bye. I could do that when I was young.

But now I'm old. I'm old now. I'm *old*. Twenty-two. Almost 23."

"You can do a 3,000," Bowman says cajolingly.

"I won't do it," Phelps says, with a defiant shake of the head.

Bowman turns toward him. He's still smiling, but the smile has tightened. "You *will* do a 3,000."

"Absolutely not," Phelps says, heading into the restaurant. "I don't do what he says 100 percent of the time," he adds over his shoulder. "That's when he gets mad."

It's not Felix and Oscar exactly, because the odd clash over timed 3,000s aside, there's little antagonism. Since 1996, when they first encountered each other at the North Baltimore Aquatic Club, where Phelps was a talented but almost uncontrollable age-group swimmer and Bowman was the new, whip-cracking coach, there has been love and there has been loathing (not always in that order), but most of all there has been mutual respect. It's as though they're a pair of rally racers. Phelps is the driver, piloting a futuristic vehicle with an outsized engine and sick lines; Bowman is the navigator, unfurling computer models of the most efficient routes and best road conditions, knowing precisely which map has the most accurate topographic profile.

So it's surprising to learn that when Bowman recently named a horse after a swimmer, it wasn't Phelps but rather his teammates the Vanderkaay brothers. How come? "Well, Number 1, that's a lot of pressure to put on a horse," Bowman says. "And Number 2, this horse is too nice. The one that bites me I'll name Michael."

IV. THE PLAN

The fake Michael Phelps stands on the block above lane 1—and here we have a problem. He has been hired as a stand-in for a PowerBar TV commercial being shot at an indoor pool in Commerce, Calif., and though his hair, at least, is identical and he swings his arms convincingly while 45 technicians adjust the lighting, the real Phelps would never, ever be starting a race from the outside lane.

Actually, at this moment the real Phelps is crammed into a jerry-rigged sound studio in the pool's sauna, fully clothed in low-slung blue jeans, flip-flops and a PowerBar T-shirt. On his head is a Dodgers cap jammed down and backward. He yawns broadly.

"O.K., Michael," the director, standing next to him, says. "Project. Not exactly anger, but we need more energy. You're on the starting blocks. Intense. We need intense."

"They say I should be afraid because every swimmer in the water is out to get me," Phelps says, sounding slightly menacing. He pauses for a beat. "Fear is good."

"Down a little in register," the director commands, "almost as if you're whispering."

"*Fear* is good. Fear is *good*. Fear *is* good." Phelps gamely repeats his lines, with different inflections. Though perfectly serviceable, his delivery does not hint at a future acting career.

In the hallway behind him, a PowerBar executive turns to Marissa Gagnon, one of Phelps's agents from Octagon. "This is kind of a lot for him to do," he says,

acknowledging the 15-hour workday that Phelps is putting in on the heels of a four-day competition, the PowerBaralooza of promotional duties that are part of the deal for an athlete whom CNBC has dubbed Madison Avenue's Golden Boy. Gagnon smiles. "Oh, he loves it," she says.

It's not really a lie. And even later, five hours into the shoot at 10 p.m., when Phelps is handed six sheets of questions that need to be answered on camera so they can be aired at PowerBar's next corporate sales meeting—What are your goals? How do PowerBar products help you achieve your goals?—he remains an affable and polished pro.

It wasn't always this way. Certainly, Phelps can be forgiven for stumbling through his earliest press conferences. He was, after all, 15—and a young 15 at that, a gawky kid struggling with his parents' divorce. At swim meets he threw tantrums and goggles. In practice and in life he chafed at Bowman's relentless discipline. For all the credit due his mother, Debbie; his older sisters, Hilary and Whitney (both successful swimmers); and Bowman, the main architect of Phelps 2.0 has been his agent, Octagon's Peter Carlisle.

When they met in 2001, Phelps told Carlisle that he wanted nothing less than to "change the sport of swimming." Carlisle listened. And it's likely that Octagon's handling of Phelps's career will be a model for future Olympians. As Phelps headed into Beijing, he was already a seven-figure industry—a first for any swimmer—with sponsors that, along with PowerBar, included AT&T, Omega watches, Speedo, Visa and the language software company Rosetta Stone. (And, yes, Phelps was using that last company's products to learn Mandarin.)

Carlisle's tour de force came in 2003. Reasoning (correctly) that a splashy pre-Athens deal linked to Spitz's seven golds would set off a media jamboree, he got Speedo to agree to a million-dollar bounty for at least equaling that number. And with that, Phelps's goal was largely realized. Because in this country nothing raises the profile of a sport like a couple of commas on a check.

V. THE SUIT

If there was ever a low-tech sport, you'd think it would be swimming. You've got water; you've got the human body. But wait: There's the suit. And when an unclipped fingernail can mean the difference between gold and not-so-gold, tinkering with this one variable makes sense. In the 1970s, female suits were stripped of the built-in skirts that scooped up gallons on every turn. Next came spandex. Throughout the next two decades suits became ever tinier, leading to visions of a suitless future in which a swimmer's privates would merely be spritzed with rubberized paint. Instead, things went the other way. Skin moves

around, people realized. It creates drag. Beginning in '96, suits expanded to cover the entire body, and suddenly there was a lot of material to work with. So why not invent a new fabric covered in denticles, like a shark's skin? Why not laminate and truss and bond zippers and weld seams and otherwise make damn sure that the contours of the human body are wrestled into sleek submission?

The zenith came in February: Speedo's LZR Racer. To call this a swimsuit is to call the space shuttle a plane. Designed with input from NASA, fluid dynamics engineers, the avant-garde Japanese designer Rei Kawakubo of the fashion label Comme des Garçons, not to mention Phelps and Bowman, its arrival rocked the swimming world. *Technological doping* and *unfair advantage* were among the responses to its core-stabilizing, vibration-reducing polyurethane compression panels. "What we're finding is that swimmers who've worn the suit have dropped two percent off their best times," Bowman says. "Which is an enormous amount." From the time of its release until the start of the Beijing Games, 48 world records were set in the LZR. And when U.S. coach Mark Schubert predicted that any swimmer not wearing it "may end up at home watching on NBC," rival companies scrambled to create similar designs, and to stave off mutiny among their swimmers, none of whom intended to leave 2% in the locker room.

VI. THE POOL

There are pools and there are pools, but for swimmers there's one question: Is it fast? Fast equals world records. Take Athens, where surprisingly few were set. The pool was outdoors, which meant sun in a backstroker's eyes and headwinds in the sprints. Worse, it was shallow. Deep water absorbs turbulence, while shallow water deflects it. Shallow can also mean warm, and the perfect race temperature is cold, somewhere in the neighborhood of 76°F.

The Beijing pool was engineered for greatness. Rumored to have cost $200 million, the Water Cube is a liquid temple in which heaviness has no place. Its very walls are ethereal, made of a translucent plastic that's only .008 of an inch thick. Though its design has simultaneously drawn raves for innovation and criticism that it's "not Chinese enough," among swimmers and coaches the verdict is in: "I've looked at the specs," Bowman says. "The venue is spectacular. It is very, very fast."

VII. THE OTHER

Personally, I don't think that what he is doing really has anything to do with what I did. I do think that what I did has a major impact on what he's trying to do. Therein lies the difference.

—MARK SPITZ to *The Arizona Republic*,
June 6, 2008

"Michael's a different person than he was in Athens," Bowman says. "In 2004 he was still this relatively young kid who was going into something we didn't know anything about. Nobody had ever done it!" The uncharted water was Phelps's Olympic schedule. Starting at the 2000 Games, a semifinal round was added, meaning that a finalist in any 50-, 100- or 200-meter event now races three times rather than two. There were nights in Athens when Phelps, still reeling from the finals of one race, was herded from the warm-down pool onto the medal stand, then back to the blocks for the semifinal of another event—all in less than 30 minutes. The extra workload is just one of the reasons that comparing Phelps with Spitz is impossible. It's beyond apples and oranges; it's more like apples and PowerBars.

While Spitz represented the cutting edge of his era, he swam without cap or goggles and in full, mustachioed splendor. Phelps will be shaved down to the last follicle and be as aerodynamic as a fuselage, and he'll be able to see, but even those advantages are offset by the depth of the competition and the scalding, Testarossa speed that defines 21st-century swimming.

Then, consider that in Munich, Spitz raced 13 times, including in four individual events—freestyle and butterfly sprints, with the 200 as his longest distance. In Athens, Phelps raced 17 times, in five individual events, in all four strokes, at distances up to 400 meters. And in Beijing, Phelps's schedule will again require him to swim 17 times, in the 100 and 200 butterfly, 200 free, 200 and 400 IM and three relays. As for career longevity, Spitz swam in two Games, a disappointing 1968 followed by the triumphal '72. Phelps made his debut in Sydney, then dominated Athens and isn't half finished. "I'll go one more," Phelps says, meaning that after Beijing he's up for London in 2012. The Spitz-Phelps competition is neat, and it's sexy. But with all due respect, it's already over.

VIII. THE MOMENT

Eight years ago Phelps dived into the water for his first Olympic race. Since then he has had eight years of training, eight years of planning, eight years of waiting. Eight years to grow in every conceivable way. And we know this: Michael Phelps will be more ready than he has ever been. When the swimming begins, he will walk to his block and wipe it with his towel. He'll be listening to hip-hop, and then he will stop. He'll snap his arms three times, and his mind will slip into that instant, and everything else will fall away. And as he stands on the block he'll glance at that cross on the bottom of the pool, and it will look oddly pristine to him, as though he's never seen it before. He'll step forward. He'll reach down. And then he will go. □

EIGHT

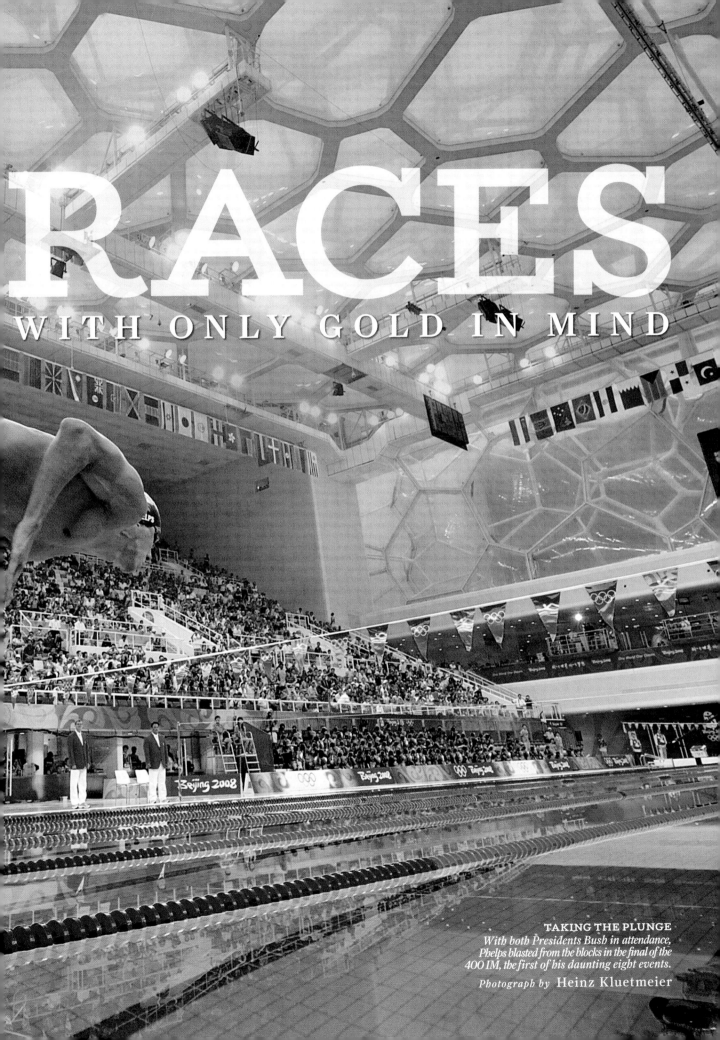

RACES
WITH ONLY GOLD IN MIND

TAKING THE PLUNGE
With both Presidents Bush in attendance, Phelps blasted from the blocks in the final of the 400 IM, the first of his daunting eight events.

Photograph by Heinz Kluetmeier

Race One

August 10, 2008

400M
INDIVIDUAL MEDLEY
4:03.84 WR

HEINZ KLUETMEIER

All eyes in Beijing turned to the pool to watch Phelps put on a four-stroke masterpiece in his first event

MIRROR, MIRROR
The fastest swimmer of them all smashed his own world record and out-touched Hungary's Laszlo Cseh, both by nearly two seconds.

Photograph by **Simon Bruty**

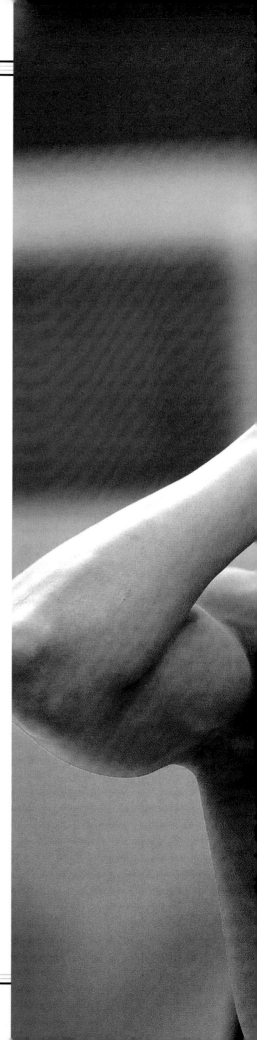

Race Two

August 11, 2008

4×100 M

FREESTYLE RELAY
3:08.24 WR

A superhuman performance from a teammate kept Phelps's golden dream alive and kicking

READY FOR TAKEOFF
First in the pool for the U.S. on the opening leg, Phelps touched second, putting his team .27 of a second behind Australia's record pace.

Photographs by **Heinz Kluetmeier**

Race Two

4 × 100M
FREESTYLE RELAY

FRENZIED FINISH
*On the anchor leg Jason Lezak (far left)
chased down France's Alain Bernard,
sparking jubilation for Phelps and
teammate Garrett Weber-Gale.*

Photographs by **Bob Bukaty/AP** *(above)*
and **John W. McDonough**

Race Three
August 12, 2008

200M
FREESTYLE
1:42.96 WR

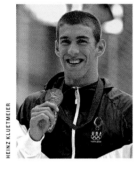

HEINZ KLUETMEIER

In one of his stronger events, Phelps sailed. Result: three races, three golds, three world records

RIGHT ON SCHEDULE
Phelps was a body length ahead of the field midway through the race, then powered to the finish, trimming his world record by nearly a second.

Photograph by **Simon Bruty**

Early Warnings
PREDATOR

No record was safe, nor was any swimmer's lead, during the opening weekend of the Games as Michael Phelps went deep into his own head to push his body into uncharted waters

by SUSAN CASEY

Photograph by Heinz Kluetmeier

MICHAEL PHELPS could see it clearly, even from 50 meters away. On the final lap of the men's 4 × 100 freestyle relay the U.S. was in second place, almost a body length behind France. As the French anchor, Alain Bernard, powered off the turn and headed for the finish, a grand Gallic victory seemed inevitable. Bernard, after all, is a rocket of a guy, a 6' 5" 25-year-old who broke the 100 freestyle world record twice last spring and whose nickname is the Horse. Though the American anchor, three-time Olympian and veteran sprinter Jason Lezak, 32, is no couch potato himself, to overtake Bernard he would have to temporarily become superhuman. It was a lot to ask.

For Phelps, there was nothing to do but watch as his dream of eight gold medals circled the drain on Aug. 11. As the relay lead he'd hit the wall second, but it had taken a world record to beat him, Australia's Eamon Sullivan touching first in 47.24. Phelps's split of 47.51 was a mere one one-hundredth of a second over Bernard's world record heading into the Games; only a handful of men have ever broken 48 seconds—and all but one of them were swimming in this race. The French team was strong, it was deep and, in the view of many, it was favored. Used to be, at the Olympics the Americans won this relay all the time. But then in Sydney in 2000 they were beaten by the Australians and had to settle for silver, and in Athens four years later, a bronze, the result of a drubbing by South Africa and being touched out by the Netherlands. Now it looked as though they'd have to wait another four years to regain this crown and that Phelps would be heading back to Baltimore with at least one medal that was the wrong color.

IN THE FISHBOWL
Every aspect of Phelps's quest was analyzed, from the water flow over his sleek body to his glycogen levels.

But then Lezak did something we all dream of seeing when we watch the Olympic Games: He pulled off a miracle. He regained the lost ground, pulling even with Bernard at the 95-meter mark, and then he had a perfect finish, his hand tripping the timer without the slightest deceleration. Still, it was impossible to call, and for a split second in the adrenaline haze no one knew what had happened. Phelps, bent over the block, screaming like a banshee, looked up at the clock. His teammates Garrett Weber-Gale and Cullen Jones did the same. Every pair of eyes in the stadium took it in: The Americans had beaten the French by .08 of a second.

And then Phelps leaned back and roared, all clenched fists and tendons; all the joy and all the pain and all the relief distilled into one epic moment. Lezak had swum the fastest split in history, 46.06 seconds, almost seven-tenths faster than that of Bernard. The Americans had gouged four seconds out of the world record, lowering it from 3:12.23 to 3:08.24.

This was not just fast; this was a new definition of fast. And for swimming, the stakes had never been higher.

THESE WERE the nine days that Michael Phelps had been waiting for, planning for, training for; and in the weeks leading up to Beijing, the world had been waiting to watch it happen.

At 6:30 on the evening of Aug. 9 the competition began: 894 swimmers from 162 countries, a global convention of V-shaped backs. There were battalions of coaches and squadrons of officials, legions of blue-

shirted volunteers and a quartet of dancing mascots, all slipping around on the white-tile deck. There was a pair of petite Chinese girls perched side by side on lifeguard chairs ready to spring to the rescue, should it come to that. Every camera angle was manned, every press seat occupied. Some 11,000 people filled the stands as the heats of the men's 400-meter individual medley, the Games' first swimming event, hit the water.

In this first of his 17 races at these Games, Phelps set an Olympic record of 4:07.82. But that was only a teaser, an amuse-bouche of sport—more than 2.5 seconds slower than his world record of 4:05.25. During the next morning's finals Phelps shattered both, in a blazing 4:03.84.

Watching Phelps on the medal podium waving to his mother and President Bush, alternately moved to tears, joking with bronze medalist and close friend Ryan Lochte and laughing when the national anthem was suddenly cut short (apparently we are no longer the home of the brave), you'd never have known that he'd just put up the fastest time in history in a race that swimmers consider the ultimate in gut-churning pain. (Phelps himself admits that "the last 50 of a 400 IM, I'm thinking, *Please, God, let me get to this wall.*") Certainly you wouldn't guess that before the race Phelps had felt crummy, beset by what he called "cold chills." Rather, he looked invigorated. And if in the next day's 200 freestyle preliminaries he cruised through to the semifinals nearly three seconds off his world-record time, then ended those semis in uncharacteristic fourth place a day later, no one was really that concerned. For Michael Phelps, the real business is done in the finals.

THOUGH PHELPS tends to make winning look easy, even a single gold medal performance requires any number of stars to align. Take the process of tapering, of physically preparing not only to be able to win against the world's best but also to do it at exactly the right moment, at an event that occurs once every four years. This, as one might imagine, is diabolically complicated. "When you taper swimmers for a meet, it's like getting a haircut," says Bob Bowman, Phelps's coach of 12 years. "You never know if it's any good until it's too late." The competitor needs to be deeply rested but not so much that fitness is lost; loose, but with all of his edge. And there's no one-size-fits-all method: Everyone peaks differently. Phelps's ideal race preparation, for instance, might destroy another swimmer.

Before the rest can begin, however, maximum performance first demands maximum training—in other words, for the tapering to work, there must be work from which to taper. In Phelps's regime, this is not a problem. Bowman has a Marquis de Sade knack for adding twists of difficulty to his workouts, things like hypoxic train-

FOCUSED
A vital part of Olympic success lies between the ears, and Phelps has a singular ability to clear his mind of clutter.

ing, during which swimmers may turn their heads for air only at certain points during a lap. There are grueling sets of 30 × 100-meter repeats that require Phelps and his teammates to hoist themselves out of the pool at the 50-meter mark and then start the remaining 50—the butterfly—from the blocks. (Climbing out of the water over and over adds an extra aerobic component to a regimen that's already doing just fine in that department.) "It's horrible," Phelps says, shaking his head with distaste. "By number 20 you get out, you're holding on to the blocks, your head's spinning, you can't even stand up."

"One of my favorite sets," Bowman says, with a mischievous lilt to his voice. Though his other passion is training thoroughbred racehorses, the coach admits that there isn't much crossover between humans and equines: "If we trained the horses like we did the people, we'd kill them."

YET FOR all the emphasis on an athlete's body, a large part of Olympic success lies between the ears. By the time an Olympic swimmer emerges from the ready room and walks out on deck to stand behind his block, the equation is far more than physical. He's spelunking deep into his psyche, emptying his mind of all the clutter. He is singularly focused. "I try to go into my own little world," Phelps says. And though, like Phelps, a swimmer may be momentarily accompanied in that world by Young Jeezy or Jay-Z, when the headphones come off, the only voice he's left with is the one inside his head. And that voice can be friend or enemy.

During the 4 × 100 final, for example, Lezak recalls, "I saw how far ahead [Bernard] was, and it crossed my mind for a split second: There's no way." But in the next instant he was able to scratch that and replace it with, "This is the Olympic Games. I'm representing the United States of America."

If Phelps entertains any self-doubt during races, it isn't apparent. "This is the thing I love the most," he says. "I love to race." When Phelps talks about competing, his entire energy field changes. He morphs from laid-back dude into quietly ferocious predator. There is no braggadocio in this. It's simply the knowledge that his talk is firmly backed up by results, the same kind of certainty one would expect when hearing, for instance, Tiger Woods holding forth on chip shots.

"That's why I'd never let him go to a sports psychologist," Bowman says. "You don't want anybody messing with that."

Along with the physical, psychological and emotional considerations of swimming, toss in a few technological ones, which play an increasingly important role and which are at least partly responsible for the sport's constant parade of world records. High in the Water Cube, tucked under the rafters, was the former South African world-record sprinter Jonty Skinner, now USA Swimming's performance science and technology director. While the Phelps camp likes to refer to Bowman as "the mad scientist," Skinner could also lay claim to that title.

"I'm looking at the race in terms of mathematics," he says, flanked by laptops. "How many strokes and how fast the strokes are, all about the turns, those kinds of things. Every meter in the pool is covered in terms of analysis." Camera feeds from above and below the water are also gathered, and all of this data is compiled and fed to the coaches and athletes in the warm-down area within 20 minutes of a race's completion. And then, Skinner adds, "we do a comprehensive blood analysis on them to look at what I would call the metabolic cost, the energetic cost of the performance as well as how they recover."

For Phelps, with his 17 races, recovery is key. Exertion creates lactic acid, the athletic equivalent of kryptonite, and there are perfectly legal ways to minimize its residency in the body. Longer warm-downs, for one. Three minutes after Phelps's race, or theoretically when lactic acid production is at its highest, someone will prick his ear with a needle, and that blood will be measured to see how many millimoles of muscular waste must be cleared from his system. Phelps will then swim easily until the readings drop to an acceptable level.

"We're mapping him all the way," Skinner says. "With so many races, we really want to stay on top of things to make sure he's staying on track and not getting too fatigued."

Along with these ministrations, USA Swimming has also employed fluid-mechanics experts to examine how water is most efficiently shunted over the human body. Meanwhile, Speedo has invested millions in the development of the LZR Racer, an unprecedented, swing-for-the-fences bodysuit that has been credited with more than 50 world-record swims since its debut last February.

Tinkering with the angle at which the swimmers' fingers enter the water; computing the flow mechanics of an alternate head angle; charting glycogen levels; encasing the body in polyurethane: If it seems that nothing is being left to chance, that's because, really, nothing is. Though few things make Phelps crankier than asking him to tell you his goals (which are famously secret and known only to himself and Bowman), even the sloppiest back-of-the-envelope calculation makes it clear that by declaring eight golds as his ultimate challenge—a feat that quickly moved from possible to probable after Phelps smashed yet another world record in the 200 freestyle on Aug. 12—we are thinking small. This is Phelps's third Olympiad, and he's only 23. He could have lost one or two or even three races in Beijing and still walked away with more career golds than not only Mark Spitz but also anyone, ever—and that's before you consider London in 2012, in which Phelps has said he would like to compete. "I just want to do things no one else has done," he says.

And if he doesn't realize all of his goals, whatever they might be? "He's the best ever in this sport," says Weber-Gale, his relay teammate. "Regardless of what happens." □

WHAT LIES BENEATH
When Phelps talks about competing, his entire energy field changes. He morphs from laid-back dude into quietly ferocious predator.

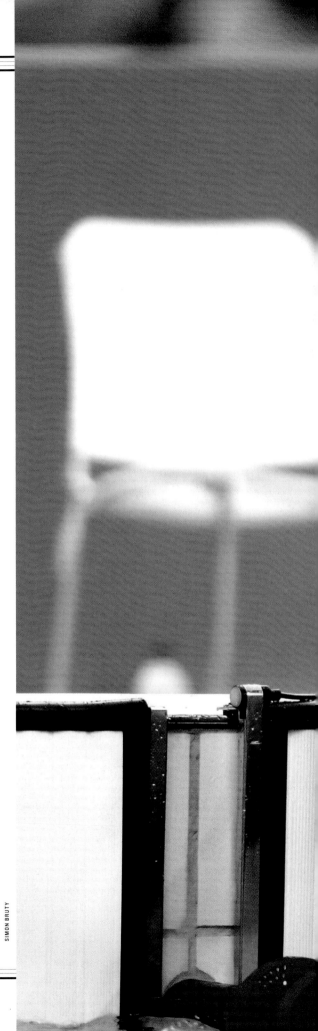

Race Four

August 13, 2008

200M
BUTTERFLY
1:52.03 WR

JOHN BIEVER

Not even a pair of waterlogged goggles could prevent Phelps from churning to yet another gold

BLIND AMBITION
The leaks had Phelps "more or less counting strokes," but he still left Mark Spitz in his mighty wake with career gold number 10.

Photograph by **Simon Bruty**

Race Five

August 13, 2008

4×200 M
FREESTYLE RELAY
6:58.56 WR

HEINZ KLUETMEIER

A mere hour after his fourth final, Phelps led off the most dominant 4×200 freestyle race ever

UNDER SEVEN? HEAVEN!
Ricky Berens, Ryan Lochte and Phelps celebrated as Peter Vanderkaay touched the wall just under the vaunted seven-minute mark.

Photograph by **Simon Bruty**

Race Six

August 15, 2008

200M
INDIVIDUAL MEDLEY
1:54.23 WR

Dubbed the American Superfish by the Chinese press, Phelps swam to an early lead and never trailed

BACK TO BUSINESS
Phelps bested the field by more than two seconds, then stuffed the gold in his pocket to make his next race.

Photographs by **Heinz Kluetmeier**

READY FOR HIS CLOSE-UP
Phelps, always technically superb thanks to relentless coach Bob Bowman, executed another turn under the ever-watchful eye of a camera.

Photograph by Heinz Kluetmeier

Race Seven

August 16, 2008

100M

BUTTERFLY
50.58 OR

PETER READ MILLER

In a race that will be remembered forever, Phelps somehow won when it looked like he'd lost

TUNING OUT THE ENEMY
Before the race, competitor Milorad Cavic suggested that a Phelps loss would be "good for the sport." Phelps's camp made sure he heard the taunt.

Photograph by **John W. McDonough**

Race Seven
100M
BUTTERFLY

BEGINNING OF THE END
As the race reached its dramatic conclusion, Phelps (left) had stormed back from seventh at the turn to close in on Cavic (right).

Photograph by **Heinz Kluetmeier**
with **Jeff Kavanaugh**

Race Seven

100 M
BUTTERFLY

HALF-STROKE OF GENIUS
*While Cavic glided to the wall,
Phelps snuck in a partial stroke. "I
thought that [last stroke] cost me the
race," he said.* Au contraire. . . .

Photograph by Heinz Kluetmeier
with Jeff Kavanaugh

Race Seven

100M
BUTTERFLY

SEE IT TO BELIEVE IT
Victory! The electronic touch pad, confirmed by SI's photos, put Phelps ahead by .01 of a second, a miraculous fingernail.

Photograph by Heinz Kluetmeier
with Jeff Kavanaugh

Race Eight

August 17, 2008

4×100M
MEDLEY RELAY
3:29.34 WR

HEINZ KLUETMEIER

With his goal in sight, Phelps helped Team USA overcome an early deficit to win historic gold number eight

BLOCK PARTY
When Phelps hit the water for the third leg, the U.S. team was in third place. But his race-best 50.15 fly split quickly remedied that.

Photograph by **Simon Bruty**

Race Eight
4×100M
MEDLEY RELAY

IT TAKES FOUR
Aaron Peirsol (top) showed his golden backstroke form in the first leg, but Brendan Hansen's breaststroke left the U.S. trailing Japan and Australia. Phelps and anchorman Jason Lezak (above), hero of the 4x100 freestyle relay, met the final challenge and rallied to win.

Photograph by **John Biever**

The Unattainable Attained

A WORLD OF BELIEVERS

By completing The Greatest Olympic Performance Ever,
Michael Phelps belongs to history, leaving us all to marvel—and
to wonder what more he will accomplish in his brilliant career

by SUSAN CASEY

Photograph by John W. McDonough

DOWN IN a basement corner of the Water Cube, everything was chaos. Michael Phelps had just won his eighth gold medal, in the 4 × 100 medley relay, and the world's press was sardined into the mixed zone, a low-ceilinged concrete gauntlet through which the swimmers pass after a race. At best the mixed zone is an uninviting place; on this historic Sunday morning it was a mosh pit of outstretched hands holding cameras and voice recorders, of bodies jammed against barricades, a media Olympics in which the main sports were pushing and shoving. And the prize? A glimpse of Phelps after he exited the pool, still dripping water and fresh with victory. Hopefully he would stop for 30 seconds and say something, anything, to answer this question:

How on earth did you pull this off?

The Australian relay swimmers came first, in full-relaxation mode, their suits pulled down from their shoulders. The Russians followed, and the great Japanese breaststroker Kosuke Kitajima strolled by, and then the crowd pressed forward as Phelps arrived in the narrow passage. Walking next to a woman holding a microphone, trailed by a television crew, he was six feet, four inches of relief, fatigue and quiet joy. His shoulders curled forward, rolling him into the question-mark posture that happens to swimmers when the back muscles take on a life of their own. Asked how it felt to be the first person to win eight gold medals in a single Olympic Games and the most decorated

DEBBIE'S BOY
Everyone wanted answers—how did it feel?—in the aftermath of his record-clinching medal, but Phelps wanted only a hug from his mother.

athlete of all time, he smiled and shrugged. "I don't know," he said. "So much emotion is going through my head. . . . I kinda just want to see my mom."

No one said it would be easy, and they were right. There were many spots where Phelps—who described the competition's nine days as "nothing but an upward roller coaster"—could've seen his ride derailed. Seventeen races in eight events, three of which were relays, meant 38 opportunities for false starts, countless chances for stroke or turn violations. Then there were the races themselves. While Phelps routed the field on numerous occasions, others were white-knucklers of the highest order. On Day 3, there was the 4 × 100 freestyle relay, which the Americans won by only .08 of a second after anchor swimmer Jason Lezak came from behind with a surreal effort, the aquatic equivalent of a distraught mother lifting a car to save her baby. On Day 5, Phelps suffered every swimmer's nightmare when his goggles filled with water during the 200 butterfly. "I couldn't see," he said, describing how he'd squinted at the T on the bottom of the pool to make his turns. He won in a world-record time of 1:52.03, but he was still disappointed: "I know I can go faster than that."

"It was kind of a heartbreak," his coach, Bob Bowman, agreed. "I thought he'd go 1:50."

On Day 7 Phelps appeared exhausted after a difficult

double in which he set a world record in the 200 IM final and less than 30 minutes later dived back in for the 100 butterfly semifinals. Though he'd raced the same schedule in 2004 at Athens, the Greeks had given him a little more time between events. In Beijing it was a different story. When the 200 IM medal ceremony ended and Phelps made his victory lap around the deck, he wasn't moving quickly enough to suit the medal hostess who accompanied him. As he paused beneath the section of the stands where his mother, Debbie, and sisters Whitney and Hilary stood, the host-

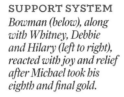

SUPPORT SYSTEM
Bowman (below), along with Whitney, Debbie and Hilary (left to right), reacted with joy and relief after Michael took his eighth and final gold.

ess (one of 337 selected in sweeps of college campuses in Shanghai and Beijing for their grace, beauty and specific proportions) reached out a silken, manicured hand and prodded Phelps firmly in the back.

"I literally had about two minutes," Phelps recalled, in which to change out of his award sweats into his race gear, tie his suit, jam his cap and goggles onto his head, stuff his gold medal into the pocket of his parka and get back on the blocks. But he won his heat, earning himself a center lane for the next day's finals.

Day 8 had started off bouncily, with nine Chinese women in white go-go boots and Nancy Sinatra ponytails drumming their hearts out on stand-up bongos. It ended with Phelps standing atop the podium wearing his seventh gold medal slung around his neck and an oddly introspective look on his face. Perhaps at that moment he was thinking about how things might well have been different.

IN THE 100 butterfly he had his closest call of all. He won the race, yes, but the margin of victory was a single hundredth of a second. Somehow Phelps had fought his way home from the back of the pack; at the 50-meter mark he'd turned seventh, .62 of a second behind the leader, Milorad Cavic, a California-born swimmer with Serbian roots who represents that country in international competition. To the topside observer, it appeared that Cavic had touched first. "He got him," Bowman said, standing on the sideline. Even Phelps's mom raised two fingers, as in: second. But . . . not. "That's why he's the King," said Russell Mark, the U.S. national team's biomechanics coordinator, of Phelps's miracle finish.

Cavic, 24, is an imposing guy with a dark and regal air, a self-described "arrogant" sprinter. He'd qualified first for this final, dropping more than a second on his personal best, and on the previous day he'd lingered in the mixed zone, holding forth about Serbia—where he has visited frequently, but never lived—and talking about the race, specifically a gesture that he'd made during the heats: a shooting motion, as though his hand were a gun. "That's ridiculous," he said, deflecting the notion that he'd been aiming at Phelps in the next lane. "If you were there, you would have seen I was firing above him, at my manager."

Perhaps he was. But he followed that by publicly stating that it would be "good for the sport" if that putative seventh gold medal went to somebody else, for instance himself. To Cavic this is standard procedure: "I enjoy a little trash-talking." Then, as the two were introduced for the final, he got right in Phelps's face.

"Go ahead," whispered a USA Swimming official, watching the exchange from the stands. "Poke the tiger with the stick."

"It's unattainable for me, and it's unattainable for anyone."
—Australian swimmer IAN THORPE, August 2004, on Phelps's chances of winning seven golds in Athens

"I have said before that I don't think he can do the eight, and I still believe that."
—IAN THORPE, August 2008, on Phelps's chances of winning eight golds in Beijing

I'VE NEVER really had a real vacation," Phelps says, considering his post-Beijing plans. "To just be on my own schedule, not have any commitments, do what I want to do, go where I want to go. You know, like,

SPLASHING!
Phelps let out a roar after his fingertip, come-from-behind victory in the 100-meter butterfly gave him his seventh win.

be free." In other words, after 12 years of grueling training, it's time for the flip side: "I'm going to sit on the beach and do nothing. I'm sleeping in. I'm putting on weight. And I'm not going to care."

Even at rest, however, Phelps's life won't be sedentary. He and Bowman had a deal: Until Aug. 17, 2008, Phelps would stick to the pool. (Admittedly less adept on land, he'd broken his right wrist last October while getting into a car.) After that date: "I'm going to do new things. I'm going to try snowboarding. I want to try golf. I'm just going to experiment." These are the kinds of plans that in the past would have struck fear into Bowman, whose sense of control is so finely tuned that a year before the 2004 Olympic trials, he had Phelps undergo a preemptive extraction of his wisdom teeth. But unless Phelps breaks a femur or two on the back nine, he'll be back in the water soon enough—with a new sheet of goals that'll likely include adding to his gold medal collection in 2012. "I think in many ways his personality is addictive," Bowman says. "He's addicted to the excitement. It's like any addiction: You have to have more, you have to have higher."

In the end the math is so pretty. At 23, Michael Phelps owns 16 Olympic medals, 14 of which are gold. But even though swimming (like all sports) is about counting—who won, who lost and by how much; how fast they went and how many strokes they took; how many medals they snagged and what color they were—there is something unquantifiable here. Something bigger. Really, what Phelps has done is disrupt the idea of *can't*. This hip-hop-listening, video-gaming pool shark; this likable guy with the generous ears who manages to seem both invincible and humble at the same time ("I'm not unbeatable. No one is unbeatable") has elevated us.

The iconic image of these Games will always be the swimmer wearing his eight-piece gold necklace, but another picture also remains: Thirty minutes before the 100 butterfly final Chinese television's raw feed had panned onto Phelps, sitting in the back row of the ready room. With its rows of white folding chairs, this room invites all the calm of a tightly packed bus en route to a mental institution. Phelps had his hands clasped on his knees, and you could see that he was breathing rhythmically, in and out, looking up and down, his eyes serious, his legs tapping with energy. In the front row the finalists in the women's 200 backstroke joked with one another and fussed with their caps and goggles, but in the back of the room Phelps was alone: early for his 16th appearance and once again left to consider the verdict that the morning would, or would not, deliver. □

HEINZ KLUETMEIER

FULL COVERAGE

A rising U.S. star before Athens in 2004, then a dominant world figure at Beijing in 2008, Michael Phelps has been a 14-time golden boy at the Olympic Games and a five-time cover boy at SPORTS ILLUSTRATED

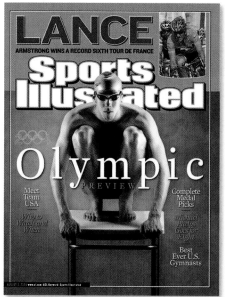

AUGUST 2, 2004

Phelps was poised to rule the pool in Athens

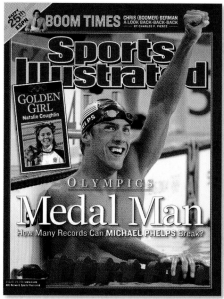

AUGUST 23, 2004

His medal count grew as records tumbled

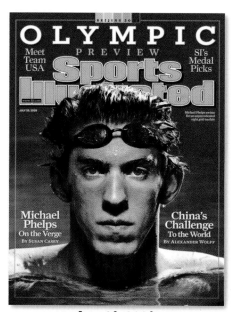

JULY 28, 2008

The inside story on his eight expectations

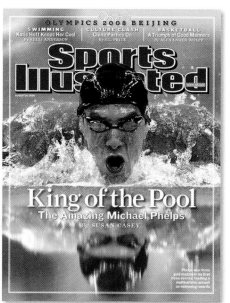

AUGUST 18, 2008

Relay magic helped Phelps splash into history

SIMON BRUTY (4); HEINZ KLUETMEIER (MEDAL MAN)

THE ALLTIME OLYMPIAN MICHAEL PHELPS

Sports Illustrated

www.SI.com

AUGUST 25, 2008

| 400 IM | WR | 4:03.84 | 4×100 FREE | WR | 3:08.24 | 200 FREE | WR | 1:42.96 | 200 FLY | WR | 1:52.03 | 4×200 FREE | WR | 6:58.56 | 200 IM | WR | 1:54.23 | 100 FLY | OR | 50.58 | 4×100 M | WR | 3:29.34 |

AUGUST 25, 2008

After one-upping Mark Spitz in Beijing, Phelps left no doubt as to who was swimming's 21st-century poster boy

The Numbers
MICHAEL'S MATH

Phelps will always be associated with the number eight,
but eight is not enough when adding up his achievements

Compiled by DAVID SABINO

Photograph by Bob Martin

16
AGE WHEN Phelps turned pro, making him the youngest U.S. professional swimmer in history.

7.18
TOTAL SECONDS by which Phelps won his five individual events in Beijing.

21.9
PERCENT OF U.S. households that tuned in to see Phelps swim for his eighth gold medal.

12,000
CALORIES CONSUMED by Phelps daily during the Olympics, nearly five times the suggested allowance for an average man.

4.37
MILES PER hour Phelps swam in setting the 200-meter freestyle world record at 1:42.96 seconds in Beijing.

26
INDIVIDUAL WORLD records Phelps has set in his career.

1.5 MILLION
FANS ON Facebook.com for Phelps, surpassing the number for Barack Obama.

87
COUNTRIES THAT won medals at the 2008 Beijing Games.

8
COUNTRIES THAT won more gold medals than Phelps (China, United States, Russia, Great Britain, Germany, Australia, South Korea and Japan).

2.1
MILES SWAM by Phelps during his 17 races in Beijing.

31
NUMBER OF the Team USA NASCAR tribute car featuring Michael Phelps and Nastia Liukin that Jeff Burton drove on Aug. 3 at Pocono Raceway.

21
POSITION that Burton finished in the race.

15,000
FANS WHO watched Phelps win his eighth gold, in the 400-meter medley relay, on the video screens at M&T Bank Stadium in Baltimore, Phelps's hometown, following the Ravens-Vikings NFL exhibition game.

$5 MILLION
ESTIMATED ANNUAL endorsement earnings for Phelps before the 2008 Olympics.

$100 MILLION
LIFETIME REVENUE that Phelps's agent, Peter Carlisle, estimated the swimmer could earn following his octet of golds.

81
PERCENT OF Match.com members who chose Phelps as the person they'd most like to be the "captain" of their "dream team."

$39.99
AMOUNT PER month Phelps would save if he takes Match.com up on its offer of a free membership.

The 200-Meter Individual Medley

6

PHELPS

VISA

WORLDWIDE SPONSOR FOR OVER 20 YEARS

The Legacy

HE'S THE WORD

In Beijing, Phelps's performance became the very definition of an unbelievable achievement

by MICHAEL FARBER

Photograph by Heinz Kluetmeier

ON A sticky Sunday morning when history and mythology were intertwined, a 23-year-old swimmer with a slack-jawed smile and an acute sense of the moment churned through lane 4 of the Water Cube and into sports immortality and the common currency of the English language. In rewriting swimming and Olympic history, Michael Phelps was rewriting the dictionary. As backstroker Aaron Peirsol, who started the 4 × 100 medley relay, would say, "The term Spitzian might be outdated now by the Phelpsian feat."

The popular term used to be Herculean—Phelps surpassed Mark Spitz's record of seven Olympic gold medals at a single Games, but how does that compare with Hercules's alltime mark of 12 labors? The Roman strongman merely had to muck the Augean stables, capture the Cretan bull and retrieve the golden apples of the Hesperides. Golden apples, gold medals. Tomato, tomahto. You tell me the grander accomplishment: completing the labors in those mythical days of B.C. or performing prodigious feats in 2008 NBC? Hercules did not have to do 17 swims in nine days, overcome a trash-talking French team in the 4 × 100 freestyle relay, battle through malfunctioning goggles in the 200-meter butterfly final, out-touch a mouthy opponent in the 100 fly by .01 or do any of this before a global audience.

Phelps did get some help from an unlikely source—Spitz himself. "It still is an amazing feat," Phelps said of Spitz's seven-for-seven in '72. "Being able to have something like that to shoot for . . . on those days when

NO SWEAT
As the world watched, Phelps made what seemed impossible look easy.

you wanted to go home and sleep [through] the workout, it made those days easier. I'd look at him [Spitz] and say, Well, I want to do this."

Phelps wrote this amazing tale, but others tell it far better. They are his Greek chorus, the ones who were only too happy to comment and bear witness. Rather than resentment at being subsumed by all things Phelps, they seemed happy to breathe in the same chlorine fumes, to warm themselves in the glow of his reflected glory.

Now the debate resumes on Phelps's proper place in the Olympic pantheon. (Did Hercules have to go through this? Hey, didn't Atlas have some serious chops?) You take Phelps, who has won a record 14 golds among his 16 Olympic medals, and somebody will raise you a Larisa Latynina, the Soviet gymnast who holds the record with 18 medals, or a Birgit Fischer, the German kayaker who started in 1980 and finished in 2004 with eight golds and four silvers while paddling single, doubles and fours, or a Carl Lewis, the U.S. sprinter–long jumper who finished first eight times and won nine gold medals (thank you, Ben Johnson) while competing in four Games.

In the overheated bubble of the Olympics, with Phelps's hair barely dry, there was an impulse to call him the greatest and be done with it. But longevity as well as accomplishment defines the best in any discipline, and Phelps could use one more productive Olympics in London 2012 to secure the top step of the podium in future barroom debates. If he focuses on the sprint—as his coach, Bob Bowman, hopes—and continues to lord over the swimming world, he would be displaying the versatility of Paavo Nurmi, the Finnish runner who won nine golds at three distances over three Olympics.

But that Greatest Olympian Ever discussion should be reserved for another day when eight-for-eight has marinated in the mind.

Once Phelps meets all the obligations of Olympic hero, he will disappear for a while. He admitted he was tired in Beijing, winning freestyles and butterflys and relays and maybe killing the Nemean Lion in his spare time. He just wants some sack time in his own bed in Baltimore. After a Phelpsian performance, he's earned it. □

The 4x100-Meter Medley Relay

VISA

WORLDWIDE SPONSOR FOR OVER 20 YEARS

Maybe it's not where an athlete's from that makes us root for them.

Maybe it's not the flag on their back, or the anthem that we hear when they win

that makes us cheer. Maybe it's simply that they are human.

And we are human. And when they succeed, we succeed.

Congratulations, Michael, and all the athletes of the Beijing Olympic Games.

GO WORLD

VISA

WORLDWIDE SPONSOR FOR OVER 20 YEARS AND
THE ONLY CARD ACCEPTED AT THE OLYMPIC GAMES

visa.com/goworld